The First Day of Kindergarten

by Tristan Horrom
illustrated by Angela Adams

Pre-Decodable 1

McGraw Hill Education

Bothell, WA • Chicago, IL • Columbus, OH • New York, NY

MHEonline.com

Mc Graw Hill Education

Send all inquiries to:
McGraw-Hill Education
8787 Orion Place
Columbus, OH 43240

ISBN: 978-0-02-145293-4
MHID: 0-02-145293-8

Printed in China

9 10 11 12 13 DSS 28 27 26 25 24